AF413254

Our Ultimate Destination

Tapasi C Saha

ISBN 979-8-3303-5183-1

Author Tapasi C Saha

Book Design Dave Turner

Cover Art *Enter Softly* by Rita J. Maggart

Published by Ingram Spark

Printed in the USA by Ingram Spark

The views expressed in this book are those of the author

and do not necessarily reflect the views

of the National Kidney Foundation.

For My Mother Sriti Kona Chowdhury

Dear Taposi,
    May the "bytes"
show you the way.
          Karl Wolph___
          June 18, 01

          [signature]
          6.18.01

Introduction

Dr. Tapasi Saha's first published book of poems, many of which have been published individually in newspaper articles and journals, is both profoundly touching and genuinely heartfelt.

Like the uniqueness of a painter's brushstroke or an entertainer's voice, Dr. Saha's poetry, published in her own unique language, carries you on an intimate journey through the defining experiences of her life as a child, medical student, physician, wife and mother.

As a devoted nephrologist and the director of two dialysis centers, Dr. Saha often becomes an integral partner in her patients' journey through life. Many of the compassionate expressions of her heart and soul found in this book, were gifts of inspiration and comfort to her beloved patients and their families.

Some of the poems in this collection are recited in Dr. Saha's own gentle voice in YouTube videos linked via a QR code at the back of this book.

It is my joy to introduce you to Dr. Saha's first collection of poems and to the heart of a healer.

Trudy Peters
Children's book author

Warm Regards

My dear friend Tapasi has the gift of writing poetry that will speak to your heart. As I reflect on our friendship, I am filled with admiration and gratitude for the beauty and depth of her words. Her poetry has a special place in my heart, and I am honored to share what her remarkable talent has meant to me.

Through the years, I have had the blessing of attending several poetry readings hosted by Tapasi. I am always astonished by the raw emotion and honesty of her poetry. She is able to paint vivid images with the written word that capture the human experience, stirring up emotions and touching the soul. When I lost my father several years ago, Tapasi wrote me a poem that perfectly expressed the loss I was feeling. Her words were light and comfort in the darkness of my unbearable grief. My heart began to heal.

I am eternally grateful for Tapasi's ability to enrich my life as a friend and poet. She is able to craft words into a masterpiece that transcends the natural world. Be prepared to have your senses awakened as you lose yourself in her unique artwork. You too, will be blessed.
Trish Berry

Tapasi's poetry brings transformation, healing, serenity and empowerment to her patients, loved ones and, to those in need.
Markalene Earles

I am so excited for my dear friend Dr. Tapasi Saha to be able to share her passion of writing poetry with everyone through this publication. Dr. Saha has been gifted with the talent for capturing feelings and transcribing them into beautiful words from the heart. Her poetry reflects her compassion and love for her family, friends, and her patients as they navigate the ups and downs of life. Cheers!
Diane Sporole

I am so proud of my dear friend, Dr. Tapasi Saha, and of the poetry gift that she is generously sharing with others in this book. She has a beautiful way of pouring her heart into every poem that she writes or recites. Her words reflect the passion that she has for life and her compassion for others. She is sharing a part of her beautiful soul in hopes of helping her patients and making this world a little more beautiful in the process.
Alisha Canter

From the Author

Mom's death shook me to my soul, the grief of losing mother was unbelievably unbearable, her memories started haunting me day and night.

Although I was living thousands of miles away from Mom, her absence in this world felt like a limb had fallen from the body, I felt so drained, so powerless.
I was desperately looking for a window to breathe out. One fine morning I started writing poetry which gave me the best comfort ever. I fell in love with poetry.

Poetries literally lift me when I am down.

Poetries wrapped their arms around me when I was distressed or sad. Poetries calm me when I weep.

Soon I realized poetry is the antidote for my stress and that poetry made me emotionally intellectual.

Initially I started writing poetry for my own comfort and later on I started writing poetry for everyone's comfort. For example if my friend's mom passed away or friend's dad passed away or any of my patients are sad I will write a poem. In these situations it always works more than you can think of.

Poetry built a flowery home in my heart and from that flowery home I pick up a flower whenever I need to.

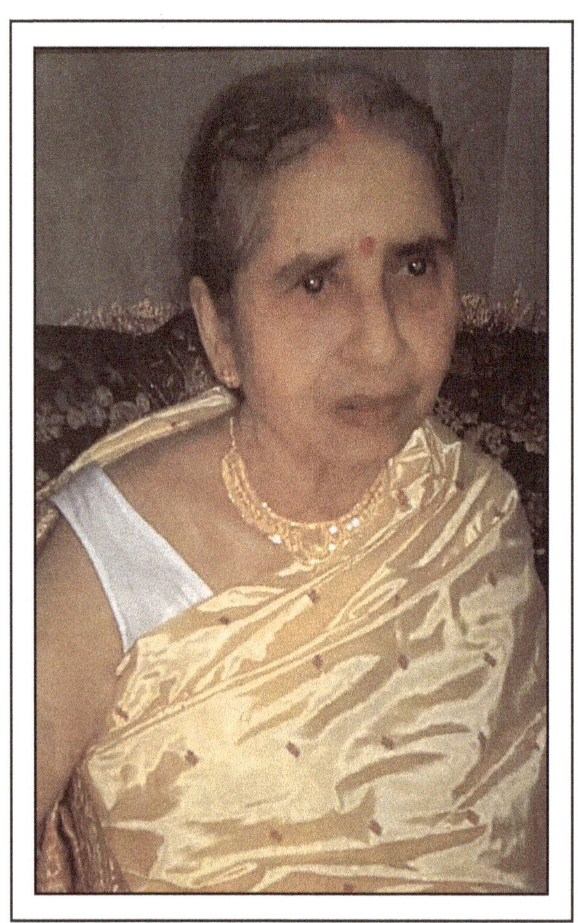

To me Ma

To me Ma means a comforting word

Or Ma means a serene peaceful sound

To me Ma means bunch of kisses on forehead

Or Ma means two lovable arms always ready to hug

To me Ma means someone who is always there for you

Or Ma means who always love you selflessly

To me Ma means a shoulder to hold on

Or Ma means whom I can trust without any doubt

To me Ma means who loves you endlessly

Or Ma means who will never ask you return her love

So to me Ma means love, lots of love, nothing but love

Letter To My Mother

To Sriti Kona Chowdhury

Mother, I am writing this letter with enormous sadness in my heart,
The 23rd of March is a special day for me, but actually
This special day brings me mixed feelings
Whenever I think about the fact that I can never see you again
My heart fills with a dark cloud, and breaks so that I can hardly breath
Missing you, I feel drained and powerless all day long
Then I remember all the pain and sufferings you endured
Happiness fills my empty heart as I know that is gone for you
But to tell you the truth I always carry you in my heart
And I always feel your presence inside my soul
When I am sad I feel that you're patting on my back
When I am happy you are my dancing heart
You were the most beautiful woman I have ever known
Mother you taught me how to love, how to care
I always think when I will be able to leave this thirsty world
And meet you in the beautiful garden of heaven where you're currently residing
I am grateful to God that on the 23rd March of 2012 he relieved your sufferings
You always loved to sing but after the stroke you became non-verbal
You always wanted to live your life with dignity
But, you had to live a life for few years that you never wanted
I barely had any meaningful conversation with you after the stroke until you passed
With the speech therapy, your speech was improved little bit
You sang your last song "Amar Bela Ja Jai" (my days are ending)
Mother you had a great husband, Daddy loved you so much so much
In my eyes the best love scene on the earth
You are sitting in the wheel chair and Daddy is combing your hair
It has been five years since you left us
But Mother it feels like I have not seen you in ages
Although, I miss you a lot
But I do not want to shed lots of tears today
Because I know someday we will be connected with soul again

(First published May 10, 2020 Kingsport Times News)

Daddy's Hand

To Bimal K. Chowdhury

When I was a little girl I used to feel so safe

Whenever I was holding Daddy's hand

When I went to the ocean for the first time holding Daddy's hand

Playing with the water soaking my dresses with water

Playing different games with the deep waves of the ocean

Never been worried how deep the water is

Never been worried that I will be drowned

Because I was holding Daddy's hand

When I was a little girl I used to feel so secure

Whenever I was holding Daddy's hand

When I was a little girl I used to feel so worry free

Whenever I was holding Daddy's hand

Because it was Daddy's hand that

Always made me feel so safe, secure and worry free

And I was always out of danger because of Daddy's hand

So it was always Daddy's hand

It was always Daddy's hand keeping me away from danger

So it was Daddy's hand

It was Daddy's hand

(First published January 21, 2018 Kingsport Times News)

Losing A Day From My Life Does Not Feel Right Doc

Inspired by a patient conversation

Losing a day from my life does not feel right Doc

Especially when someone is diagnosed with metastatic cancer

Because my days are numbered now

Tomorrow I may not be here

But to tell you the truth, I really don't want to die now

Because I have so much to live for

And I have so much left yet to do

Losing a day from my life feels painful inside

Because soon I have to leave all those I dearly love on Earth

Losing a day from my life does not feel right Doc

Because it feels like God is calling to me from heaven far above

Saying "Your time on the Earth is over"

Losing a day from my life often feel like God is asking me

"What didn't I do right when I was on earth"

Losing a day from my life doesn't feel right Doc

But the sad thing is my clock is already turned on by God

And nobody in this world has the power to stop that clock

Bradford Pears

Bradford Pears are blooming in my yard

Their enormous beauty makes me glow in and out

Their gorgeous look just takes my breath away

Their beautiful display fills my heart with joy and serenity

Their smiley faces are too adorable for words

Their angelic faces are so delightful to watch

The Bradford Pears are blooming in my yard

Bradford Pears are my happiest tears

I will be their craziest lover forever

The beauty of their innocence makes my heart brighten profusely

Seeing the Bradford pears is like breathing fresh air

Bradford Pears are my dearly peers.

I crave to see them every spring year

Deal With Your Stresses Wisely

Cut your stressors and deal with your stresses wisely
If you don't your life will be in trouble surely
If cancer is a killer stress will be the super killer
So, you need to know how to deal with the super killer wisely
There are lots of unwanted stresses around you
But always remember if somebody is hateful to you
it's their own behavioral problem not yours
So, if you have sleepless night because of someone's improper acts
That's the wrong way to deal with the stresses
If someone hurts your feelings for no reason stay away from them
If you don't they will try to hurt you again
Be honest to yourself, keep your self-esteem up
Possessing little self-esteem can lead people to become depressed
And depressed people always go in wrong direction
Some choose the dark life some take their own life
So, cut your stressors and deal your stresses wisely
Always, always try to stay calm, forget the bad memories
don't choose the wrong path that will mess up your whole life
Find a hobby for your heart and soul, for me it's poetry of course
Feed your soul with music which has soothing effects on your heart and soul
Keep yourself busy, daily exercise and yoga of course
can cut your stresses significantly
So, cut your stressors mental or social whatever it is you'll never go wrong
Deal with your stresses wisely
if you do your life will not be in trouble surely

Death Means Our Ultimate Destiny

Death means somebody snatching your heartbeat

Death means somebody draining your energy

Death means you are losing your muscle strength

Death means feeling of powerlessness

Death means you are not in your own mind

Death means somebody taking away your consciousness

Death means everything in front of you is blurred

Death means somebody taking you away from your dear ones

Death means you are craving to see your known faces

Death means you are in the dark room gasping for air

Death means you are walking on hard rocks

Death means you are desperate to see light

Death means way to heaven

Death means where we all desire to go

Finally death means our ultimate destiny

Love Means

Love means some distinct colorful dream which suddenly makes you floating in the air

Love means when your heart and soul yearn for someone

Love means when you're looking out the window thinking about your dear one

Love means immortal connection between two souls

Love means merging of the two pair of lips

Love means drowning deep into the ocean

Love means woefully perfect addiction

Love means enormous silence and emptiness in the chest

Love means indefinite destination

Love means longing of your heart to see your sweetheart

Love means emotional storm

Loves means harmony between two hearts

Love means unconditional trust between two souls

Love means inevitable attraction between two people

Finally, Love is such a powerful word no words are enough to define it!

Desire

I wish I was a bird that's the longing of my heart since my childhood

I wish I was a bird moving through the clouds

with a great desire merging with the monstrous earth

I wish I was a bird flying over the clouds

floating with the winds fighting with the storm

to meet my mate across the world

I wish I was a bird flying over one tree to another

with immeasurable energy and pride

I wish I was a bird so that i do not need to care for anyone on earth

I wish I was a bird crossing over a crowd

without caring what they are fighting about

I wish I was a bird so that I can soak my mind and soul

with water on a rainy night

I wish I was a bird so that I can recite with enormous pride

and sing with most magnificent soul of the earth

Hey Spring Morning

Hey Spring you're surprisingly stunning this morning

Dogwood flowers started blooming my heart is pounding

Gorgeous Daffodils are so alluring so fascinating

Bradford Pears started giggling what a phenomenal morning

Hey Spring you're surprisingly astounding in the beginning

So, my mind is smiling my heart is dancing

Beautiful birds are singing what a super glorious morning

Stone in my chest melting "Oh Spring" you're astonishing

What a beautiful spring morning surprisingly stunning

Everything is blooming how amazing how amazing

During the whole winter I carry stone in my chest

Because no flowers are blooming, everything was dying

And I am badly waiting, waiting and waiting for "You Spring"

But now everything is blooming stone in my chest melting

feeling absolutely amazing, amazing and amazing

"Hey Spring" at times you're overwhelming

Bringing me all kinds of pollen allergies but I have forgiven you

considering you "Queen of the all seasons"

But Hey Spring one thing I have to admit for sure

Most of the time you're absolutely breath taking

So, my love for you never ending

HM Voice (Music Company of Bangladesh)

Listen oh listen there is a magnificent voice around

which is HM voice please love this voice

Because it's your voice it's my voice it's HM voice

This voice will melt your heart instantly

As you listen to this voice, you'll feel peace surrounding you

So, you all should listen to this voice and subscribe this voice

Because it's an authentic voice it's a fascinating voice

It's a glorious voice it's a melodious voice

It's a voice once you hear, you'll keep listening

So, you all should listen to this voice and subscribe this voice

Because it's an addictive voice it's a nostalgic voice

And this voice will bring back all of your old sweet memories

So, you all should listen to this voice and subscribe this voice

Because this voice comes from the core of your heart

This voice comes from the core of my heart

So, it's your voice it's my voice it's lovely HM voice

HM Voice is a voice which will feel your heart with joy

It's a voice which will feel your heart with comfort

This voice will take away all of your sadness and fill your heart with lots of madness

So, listen oh listen there is a magnificent voice around which is HM voice

Please listen to this voice and subscribe this voice

Because this voice is absolutely a charming voice

And it's your voice it's my voice it's lovely HM voice

I'm A Woman I love To Brag About That Fact

3-8-19 (Happy National Women's Day)

I'm a woman, I love to brag about that fact

let's rephrase, I'm a woman, I have a lot to be proud about that fact

I'm a woman, I implanted a huge tank of love inside my soul

I give away love without thinking about the fact that

whether I will get back even little bit of that

So I'm a woman, I always give away love and I admire myself for that fact

I'm a woman, I love that fact reasons are numerous of course

Forgiveness is my religion, I forgive people even when God does not want to forgive

I'm a woman, I love the fact I can play multiple roles in life

and I know how to keep everybody in right track

So I'm a woman, I absolutely love that fact

I float with enormous happiness when I give birth a new life

and I engage myself to raise that life with lots of love and care

I'm a woman, I love to brag about that fact because I'm the one

who cares about Underprivileged people, deprived people and socially abused people

I always try my best to keep the world happy and peaceful

So I'm a woman, I want to brag about that fact

Hold on Poetry

When you lost the hope of your life hold on poetry

When your life put you in a dark room hold on poetry

When the dawn coming all over your mind hold on poetry

When your dearest folks all of a sudden start hating you

For no reason hold on poetry, just hold on poetry

When your closest family all of a sudden start ignoring you

For no good reason you just need to hang on poetry

Because poetry does not betray you

Poetry does not hold you accountable for anything

Poetry only gives you lots of comfort and peaceful thoughts

Poetry does not have any expectation from you

And when there is no expectation the love is solid and selfless

So just hold on poetry whenever your life is devastated

When all of a sudden you found out one day

Your loved one has incurable disease

Just hold on poetry, hold on poetry and hold on poetry

Because poetry will help you remain serene

When your life is traumatized and dark

When your soul is overwhelmed and disturbed

So please hold on poetry, cherish the poetry

Because you will never ever go wrong holding poetry

Non-compliance

What does it mean by non-compliance?

Non-compliance means disobeying medical advice

Non-compliance means destroying God given precious life,

or unknowingly ending your life

Non-compliance is a deadly curse

Basically, it means the Inappropriate attitude towards life

Non-compliance means jumping in the pond without knowing how deep the pond is

Non-compliance means force yourself to be Gods unwanted child

Non-compliance means death is imminent

Non-compliance means walking towards dark fortune

Non-compliance means drowning in the ocean of denial

Non-compliance means drowning in the ocean of insecurity

Non-compliance means stepping on your own feet,

harming yourself without any solid reason

Non-compliance means disrespecting your oneself,

intentionally disfiguring your God given beauty

Non-compliance means inviting health hazards and getting very close to the danger zones

Non-compliance means anticipation for grand Invitation from the death city president

Non-compliance means waiting for the death city doorbell to ring

Non-compliance means depriving yourself from the companies of your love ones

Non-compliance means depriving yourself from God's blessing

Non-compliance means anticipation for dark fortune

Non-compliance means jumping in the fire before one's designated time

Sophisticated Peers

Stay away from your sophisticated peers

Because they hurt you they cut you

They tear you apart

They are your sophisticated peers

They hug you they kiss you

And they call you dear

Only if they need you badly enough

They are your sophisticated peers

They push you they pinch you

They throw you far

When they accomplish their work

They are your sophisticated peers

They constantly bug you and annoy you

And they pretend they love you

Only when they want their work to be done

They are your sophisticated peers

But ultimately, they pierce your heart

And that wound will never heal enough

Little Things Mean A Lot

Little things mean a lot we just often don't realize that

A little bit of love can make sad heart grin ear to ear

Only few caring words can change someone's life

Just a simple hug can bring warmth to someone's heart

Little bit of assurance can help someone look forward

Little bit of smiles can make sad heart giggles

Little bit of laughter can make someone move forward

Little bit of support can give someone new life

Giving little bit of happiness to others does not cost any penny

But surely bring lot of serene feelings to others

but we often forget that we often forget that

Please believe in palliative care which brings hope to others

Because little bit of smiles can change someone's whole world

And if you can put smiles on distressed face you'll never regret

In fact, you will feel so much peace inside so much comfort inside

Because little things mean a lot we just often don't realize that

Our Prayers Should Be

Our prayers should be before our days are ending

Please God take away the deaf darkness of our mind

Fill our mind with pure serenity and show us the path of light

Our prayers should be before our days are ending

Please God give us the wisdom to understand the fact

That all human being should be treated with respect

Regardless of their color and race

Because there is only one God

We are just taking different route to reach the same God

So, our prayers should be before our days are ending

Please God give us the sensibility and intelligence

So that we could tolerate and treat others better

Our prayers should be before our days are ending

Please God fill our heart with lots of love

Because love can only bring more love

And hatred can bring only more hatred

So, we should all learn to hate hatred

Also, dear God please give us the power of understanding

That if somebody hate us that will be their problem

We should be content that we do not grow hatred in our heart

In the end, our final prayers should be

Spread out our selfless love all over the world

To Me Rabindranath Means

Dedicated to Rabindranath Tagore, a famous Bengali writer

To me Rabindranath means

Hope of the heart when I am lost

Or the solace when I am distressed

To me Rabindranath means

Bunches of magnificent thoughts and vibrant emotions

That'll take me far away from all worries and bad memories

To me Rabindranath means supreme thoughts

The thoughts which has intense purity and innocence

As you go through these divine thoughts

You will feel like your whole body is purified

To me Rabindranath means the spectacular thoughts

That'll melt every corner of your heart

To me Rabindranath means

Light of the soul or joy of life

Or little cute bird singing in my heart

To me Rabindranath means

Sitting on my hubby's laps listening to love songs

To me Rabindranath means

Palliative thoughts that can ease my sorrows

And alleviate my pain and sufferings

To me Rabindranath means

Thoughts that propel me dancing in the rain

Rather than sitting in the dark room when I am down

Rabindranath means feeling proud being a woman

Finally to me Rabindranath means

Glorious history of Bengali literature

The Kind Of Love I Adore

The kind of love I adore that has purity and respect

The kind of love I adore that has honesty and comfort

The kind of love I care that does not judge me

The kind of love I desire to have which has soothing effect on my mind and soul

The kind of love I am eager to have which has divine clarity

The kind of love I love to nurture which has endless peace

The kind of love I want to feed my soul with which has forgiveness

The kind of love I want to breed inside my soul that has selflessness

The kind of love I want to breed inside my soul which is free of hatefulness

The kind of love I adore that has plenty of thoughtfulness

The kind of love I adore that has no narrowness no shallowness

filled with lots of goodness nothing else matter of course

The kind of love I adore that has purity and respect

You

I work the whole day until dawn

I fly all over the place year round

But I don't feel good when I come home

If I don't see you around

Because I wouldn't be who I am

If you didn't come into my life all of a sudden

You built me, you raised me, whoever I am

Your passion and compassion carried me this far

Your love holds me up when I am hurt

Your lap gives me heavenly comfort when I am sad

Your shoulders are my lifelong shelter

So, after a long day at work when I come home

I look around, I look around and I look around

And I don't feel good if I don't see you around

(First published February 14, 2021 Kingsport Times News)

Ups and Downs

When there are no ups and down in our life what does it mean?

It means we have reached the end of the day

When there are no ups and downs in our life what does it mean?

It means we are about to surrender our life

When there are no ups and Downs in our life what does it mean?

It means we are about to watch sundowning of our life

When there are no ups and Downs in our life what does it mean?

That means our days are declining or

We are about to reach the down slope of our life

When there are no ups and downs in our life what does it mean?

That means we are about to watch storm coming towards us

And we can see our shadow in the dark

When there are no ups and Downs in our life what does it mean?

That means our life is now laying on the flat line

Which means we are not anymore

Thirteenth of February

Dedicated to my son Upal Saha on his Birthday

I woke up this morning with tremendous joy in my heart

Do you all like to know why? Because it's thirteenth of February

I wake up every year this day with heavenly feelings inside

Do you all like to know why? Because it's thirteenth of February that's why

To me god's given all the days of the year are gifted

But thirteenth of February is a super-gifted day

because this day somebody special came in this world

to bless me with a lovely sound " hey mom "

As soon as I had him in my lap, I had forgotten all the pain

I had to go through during delivery and labor

That special boy is my son Upal Saha

Who gave me heavenly joy since his birth until now

with a lovely sound "hey mom I am here"

So, until the last day of life my ears will be eager

to hear that lovely sound "hey mom I am here"

Feels So Good When You

Dedicated to my beloved

Feels so good when you touch me with love
Feels so good when you lay by my side
Feels so good when I sit by your side you instantly ask me,
"Who is going to hold my hand?"

Feels so good, when you religiously kiss me every morning before you leave for work
Feels so good when I'm screaming looking at a new flower in the garden
you look at me with love and giggle so hard
Feels my heart with joy when you suddenly embrace me from behind
Feels so good if our common patient ask you do you know other Saha?
Your answer is yes, she is my permanent girlfriend

Feels so good some weekends when both of us are off, you kiss my eyes to wake me up
Feels so good, when you're listening a song and suddenly you start screaming
Honey, Honey come quick sit in my lap listen to this beautiful song

If some reason I'm mad with you I stop talking with you
Feels so good, when you keep asking me when the punishment will be over?
Feels my heart with joy when you hold my hand when I am crossing the road
Feels so good if I'm sad for some reason you say, "rest your head on my chest
you will feel instantly great. "

Occasionally when you have down time at work, you repeatedly text me
Feels really really good
If I ask you, "do you really need me", you say, "I always need you"
Sometimes when am doing something important and you keep disturbing me
Then I tell you "Can you not disturb me I'm doing something important."

Feels so good when you say
If I sit by a flower I can't hold myself touching it
Feels so good when you touch me with love
Feels so good when you lay by my side

(First published February 14, 2021 Kingsport Times News)

Half Soul's Agony
Dedicated to my dear friend Shannon

My beautiful wife is waiting for the last day of her life
She is now in hospice care which means end of life care
My beautiful wife is facing a life limiting illness
She is now in hospice care which means end of life care
Soon she will be gone to a place from where nobody can ever return
Soon my life will be lifeless, worthless, pointless and meaningless
We have been together for so many years
it seems like we are one body one soul so how can we be apart?
My beautiful wife is suffering from an incurable disease
She is now in hospice care which means end of life care
After few days she will be a departed soul
without her I will be walking with a heavy stone on my chest
and a shady darkness will always surround me like snakes
Somewhere deep in my heart a sad bird keeps saying
"Beautiful" please don't leave me alone, please don't leave me alone
Who is going to hold my hand when I am about to stumble
Who is going to give my smile back when I am disheartened and sad
Who is going to kiss my eyes when I am asleep?
"Sweet heart" your ceaseless love always takes me far away from earth
in a heavenly garden where I'm putting flower in your long-braided hair
"Darling" I seem to have loved you in numberless times and forms
in life after life forever so how can we be apart?
And without you there will be no meaning of my life

Heart Felt Hefty Mind Said Sadly Bye Baby

Dedicated to my son Dipaul Saha

Leaving you baby at the dormitory was not easy
Leaving you Baby at the dormitory was tough really
Somehow, I had mixed feelings I was joyful but tearful
Leaving you Baby at the dormitory was not easy
But it was necessary Baby to lift you up to see you rise
Leaving you at the dormitory was not easy
It felt like I was leaving my precious boy up there
Heart felt hefty mind said sadly "bye Baby"
Seventeen years passed by so easy
My little boy grew up so fast and easy
Leaving you Baby so far it was really hard
But I feel comfort knowing that I raise you right
Although I will miss you day and night
But I always like to see you happy and loved
Leaving you Baby at the dormitory was not easy
My mind felt soupy as if was sitting in a lonely valley
Emptiness in our nest, emptiness in my chest was hugging me so bad
Leaving you Baby at the dormitory was not easy
But it was necessary to lift you up and see you rise
Heart felt hefty mind said sadly" bye Baby
wishing you all the best as you begin your new journey"

Dear Kazi Nazrul Islam
(National Poet of Bangladesh)

I am writing this letter
And thinking about you
What do I do with you
You're always with me one way or another
Either I am with your idealism
Or I am with your theory of Humanism
I love you fully
And you're all over the places in my mind
I fell in love with you after I read your poem "Women"
Your poem taught me self-respect
Your poem showered me with self esteem
You inspired me to come out of veil
And you asked me to show the world my ability as woman
So how can I live my life without you
I can see your shadow all the time in my life
And I perform for you in my dream
Because I love you extreme
I have never seen you in my life
But your picture in the middle of my heart
So, what do I do with you
You're my soul mate
You're my first morning rose
You're my endless love
Without you I see everything dark
Today is 25th May
And it's your birthday
Which is a very precious day for me
Wish you all the best, love and respect
And millions of Pronam on your special day
"With love and regards"
Tapasi C Saha

Anoushka's Finger

Dedicated to Anoushka Shankar
(Famous Sitar Artist)

Anoushka's Finger talks without vocal cord

The divine melody she creates with her fingers

is unbelievably intoxicating, absolutely electrifying

which pierces our soul immediately

Listening to her Sitar takes us to a place

where no one else matters

When it comes to creating music

Anoushka's fingers are sharper than Shark teeth

The sharpness of her fingers only you can compare

with Goddess Ma Kali's Sword

The delicate melody she creates with her fingers

Takes us above the cloud where we're free like a bird

The musical art she creates with her fingers

melts your heart instantly fills our soul with purity

and surely brought us happy tears

The beautifully haunting musical art she creates with her fingers

One life is not enough to adore this magical blessing

Anoushka's Finger talks without a vocal cord

The divine melody she creates with her fingers

Hypnotically super beautiful musical art

It's The Sixteenth Of June

Dedicated to Dr. Karl Nolph The Pioneer of Peritoneal Dialysis

It's sixteenth of June, It's sixteenth of June
I woke up in the morning
My head feels heavy
My heart feels sorely
My mind feels blurry
Because it's sixteenth of June, It's sixteenth of June

It's sixteenth of June it's sixteenth of June
I woke up in the morning
My head feels soggy
My heart feels soupy
My mind feels muggy
Because it's sixteenth of June, It's sixteenth of June

It's sixteenth of June 2014 it's sixteenth of June 2014
Something unpleasant happened in this world
Dr. Karl Nolph, "The Pioneer of Peritoneal Dialysis"
Left this world for eternity
So, on sixteenth of June my head will be always cloudy
My heart will be always sorrowful
My mind will be always gloomy
And nothing in this world could erase these feelings

I Always See Love In His Eyes

Dedicated to my hubby Pabitra Saha

I see love in his eyes
In the middle of the running
When my shoe laces about to come out
And he kneels down to tie my shoe laces
I see love in his eyes
When he wipes my sweat with his shirt in between running
I see love in his eyes
At the end of the running
When he washes my face with cold water
I see love in his eyes
When he asks me to sit on his lap
After I had a stormy day at work
I see love in his eyes
When he instinctively wraps his arm around me
When I am in the crowd or crossing the street
That's the way he is very protective
I see love in his eyes
When he says" I came home late today
because I thought you will be late"
I see love in his eyes
Whenever I sit by him and he says
"Hun who is going to hold my hand"
I see love in his eyes whenever he says
"everything comes across you blooms including me"
I see love in his eyes
After I have done a radiant performance
When everybody is bragging about me
That's my hubby who is always madly in love with me
And that love I always see in his eyes
Even after I have done a pocket size victory
So, whenever I want love I just look in his eyes
Because I know it's always there

Mother's Love Has Unbelievable Power

Tribute to my Mother: Sriti Kona Chowdhury

Mother's love has unbelievable power which is far beyond defining with words
Mother's love is the most unselfish most forgiving everlasting
and enduring love one could ever think of
Mother's love does not treat you according to your color
It's does not matter whether you're ugly or pretty
It's does not matter whether you're black or white
It's does not matter whether you're criminal or judge
Mother's love will always surround you with enormous care
Mother's love is the most peaceful love one could ever think of
Mother's love is the cool hand on your forehead when you're not feeling well
Mother's love is the most dependable shoulder to lean on
when you're unable to cope with too much stress
Mother's love is the purest love in the whole world
So never ever ignore or disrespect that special love
if you do no matter how religious you're
you'll be of course thrown into a dark swamp by your dear God
Mother is the best teacher of our life so we all owe to our mother
Mother's love is the sincerest love one could ever think of
Mother is the place where we came from so love your mother with special care
Mother's love does not change with time it'll never fade with time
it will just grow stronger and stronger with time
Mother's love will always rise and shine even when our days on earth are over
does not matter good or bad time
mother's love will be always there with compassion and care.
Depth of Mother's unconditional love is far beyond defining with words
Mother's love has God gifted power so love your mother with special care

(First published May 12, 2024 Kingsport Times News)

Mother Oh Mother What A Treasure You Are

Dedicated to Karen Vernae Fields, mother of Markalene Earles

Mother oh Mother what a treasure you are
In your daughter's hidden heart
I will cherish you till the end of my life
Thinking about you takes me far away from earth
Thinking about you makes me so peaceful and proud
Because I represent you mother
Mother oh mother it's my pleasure to describe my feelings
For you in alluring words
I have been trying to put my thoughts together
So that I can write for you the most magnificent poem
Of the whole sphere
You are such an extraordinary creation of great universe
I will be always longing for your touch
I will be always craving for your love
Nobody can take you away from the hidden garden
Of my heart because you're unbelievably precious.
Whenever my hopes and dreams have shattered
You were always there with your outstretched arm
To hold me tight so that I can move forward
Whenever I'm scared I want to hold you in my thoughts
Until my fear subsides because you are such a Power
So one thing I have taken for granted in my life
Which is Mother's love because I know I would never lose that.
Mother oh Mother I want to hold you in my memories till the end of time
As long as wind blows as long as stars shine you will be always mine
Mother oh Mother what a treasure you are
You will be in my thoughts and dreams forever

(First published May 10, 2020 Kingsport Times News)

My Baby Is Graduating

(Dedicated to Upaul Saha)

"Hey world" with a delightful mind

I want to share with you all

A big news, an incredible news

My baby is graduating

My heart is pounding

My mind is glowing

What a beautiful feeling inside

Words are not enough to capture

"Hey world" with a radiant mind

I want to share with you all

A luminous news, a vibrant news

My baby will walk the Lawn

In a matter of days

"Hey world" with a dazzling mind

I want to share with you all

A super bright news

My baby is graduating

My heart is throbbing

My mind is glittering

What an intense feeling

And its definitely breath taking

Today is not the only day
I remember you Mom

Dedicated to my mother, Sriti Kona Chowdhury

Today is not the only day I remember you mom
I remember you every single day no matter rainy or sunny day
Today is not the only day I remember you mom
Today is not the only day the cloud floated in my mind sky
Thinking about your absence
Today is not the only day I would shed tears thinking about you
You are always in my thoughts no matter what
Today is not the only day I remember your eyes
Your eyes were so gentle I do not see those eyes anymore anywhere
Today is not the only day I remember your acts
Your every act was so loving so thoughtful
Today is not the only day I remember your voice
Your voice was so soothing, so caring, so calming
Today is not the only day I remember your gentle hand on my forehead
You always can see through me you could always read my mind
You always held my hand when I was in crisis
Today is not the only remember your shoulder
Your shoulder was my fearless shelter when I needed
Your precious lessons always give me strength
To fight against the baddest and to care about saddest
You taught me the goodness the humanity in such a kind and loving way
If you tore my heart, you will see yourself sitting there with Flowers
So, I always carry you in my heart no matter I am blue or white
Today is not the only day I remember your hugs and kisses
Which was always healing medicine for me when I needed
Today is not the only day i remember you mom
I remember you every single day no matter rainy or sunny day

Words

Dear friends please use your words with care

Because words can be harsh

Words can be soft

Words can be pathetic

Words can be sympathetic

Words can be stabbing

Words can be comforting

Words can be showered with hatefulness

Words can be showered with loveliness

Words can do so many tricks

Words can make you feel graceful

Words can make you feel disgraceful

So please use your words carefully and thoughtfully

Flower

I woke up this morning, i went down to look around

all of a sudden my eyes got fixed at something

wow, wow what a gorgeous flower, so colorful and so bright

Absolutely blooming right in front of me

I picked up the flower with a great desire

I will give it to my mother

As soon as I handed the flower to my mother

Mother said "oh darling that's why i love you so much

whenever you see flower you remember me so very much"

I thought in my mind if i was a flower mother would have come down to earth

and she will say

"Darling i needed to come down because you love me awful much"

Life

Life is stressful but life is not everlasting

So enjoy every bit of it no matter what indeed

When your mind is not in peace

When Cloud is rumbling in your mind sky

and teeming rain is making your mind soupy

Embrace the sky of the poetry deeply

Within seconds your mind will start giggling

When your heart is broken

Sewing every corner of your heart with the sky of poetry

will fill your heart with joy instantly

When your mind is not in peace go out run little bit

Nature will nourish every corner of your mind within a minute indeed

When your heart is broken go out for walking

Nature will instantly heal every corner of your heart

When you feel like a bird with broken wings

Merge yourself with the sky of the poetry

Within a second you will feel strength in your broken wings again

Life is complex and stressful but life is not indefinite

waves of happiness will always run through your heart and mind

If you embrace nature and poetry in your crisis time

Independence Is An Achievement

Independence is an achievement

Because it gives us autonomy

Independence is an achievement

Because it gives us wrinkle free smiles

Independence is an enormous achievement

Because It gives us freedom from being ruled by others

Independence is priceless jewelry

Because It gives us the ability to live our life without being governed by others

Independence is an absolute achievement

Because it gives the ability of thinking on our own which makes us independent thinker

So Independence is a huge achievement for a person ,for a society and for a nation

Independence is a super power for a country

I love independence, you love Independence

we all love Independence so let's all please say together

"Happy Independence Day of USA"

Live With Pride

(Dedicated to Rhonda Castle)

When someone shower you with plenty of love

Life feels like a piece of heaven

Life feels so endearing so precious so elegantly beautiful, on the other hand

when you're drowning yourself with sadness

When you feel lost ,when you feel empty

Life feels like no more fun and time feels like stuck at same moment

So feeling loved ,feeling happy, feeling worthy

is so very important in our life

Taking your own life should not be the option for anyone no matter what

because that's not the solution

Unpacking your emotions to someone whom you truly trust is very wise

it's foolish to make bad decision in life

without discussing with the people you trust and love

Because life is the best gift from God

And you get only one life to live

So enjoy and cherish every moment of your life

And don't let go your life unchallenged

Love yourself and think deeply how your decision will affect your love one's

Live your life with pride, giving up shouldn't be the choice for anyone

Look at the flowers to uplift you when you feel at your lowest

White Flower

White flower oh white flower

My heart is pounding watching you blooming

My heart is melting away watching your enormous beauty

The purity of your color moves my heart and soul instantly

My eyes are fixed on you , the bird inside my soul started dancing crazy

Your glorious presence dispersing sunshine all over my garden

White flower oh white flower

Your brightness is as brilliant as star

The streams of love that is flowing inside my mind

is trying to come out now and saying that

White flower oh white flower

Come close to me, embrace me, kiss me

Pour your fragrance all over me

I'm madly in love with you "gorgeous"

My heart is throbbing watching you blooming

My heart is pounding watching your enormous beauty!

I Raised You To Fly

(Dedicated to my son Dipaul Saha)

I raised you to fly away from my eyes

Where you can enrich yourself

I raised you to fly away from my eyes

Where you can shine and excel yourself

And I'm sure you'll leave sparkles each and every

place you go through out your super bright career

I raised you to ride in a super huge vessel

So that you can go as far as you want to go with your career

I raised you to fly away from my eyes

Where you can brighten and improve the quality of your life

Things will not be same as you leave for college

I can't bother anyone for breakfast anymore

I can't mess with anyone for keeping their room untidy

I don't need to pick up empty water bottles from the floor

Although I don't need to do all these but still I will not feel good

Because I will miss you a lot, I will miss you a lot

But remember I raised you to fly away from my eyes

So that you can give yourself a glorious life

And I know my blessings will always make you rise

I Have Lost My Daddy

10-27-21

Hey all i have lost my daddy, I'm looking for him everywhere

Can anyone help me finding him?

Where are you daddy? Where are you hiding?

I don't want to play hide and seek game anymore

Everything is getting dark, a storm is approaching

There will be heavy rainfall soon where can I find you now?

Who is going to buy me new dresses when I do good result on test?

Who is going to praise me for my below average cooking?

Who is going to tell me "put on your hat, scarf and gloves

when you go out running in the cold"

Who is going to tell me "gurgle with lukewarm ginger water"

when I catch a cold?

Where are you daddy? Where are you?

Did I do anything bad? You can punish me but come back daddy

. Daddy you never wanted to see your little girl crying so hard

Please daddy come back I need you badly

Can you hear me daddy?

Why did you have to go so far away from me?

Whom I'm going to call daddy now?

Hey all I have lost my daddy, I'm looking for him everywhere

Can anyone help me finding him?

My Daddy A Rare Angel

Dedicated to Bimal Kanti Chowdhury

Daddy a whole year has gone since you left for heaven
In your absence things are not the same as it was before
The day God called you heaven you didn't go alone part of me went with you
I did not get to hear your voice for so long
So many feelings still unsaid unexpressed Daddy
Every time I sit to write I see the shadow of yours all over the places all over my mind
Writing is a kind of passion that always takes me to a place
where I'm surrounded by indefinite number of fond memories
Those memories with you Daddy are my golden treasure
Daddy, you had a heart of gold and that golden heart always knew how to pour love
every time I needed
I know how deeply you loved our precious Mom
I have dual feelings in my heart,
I feel joyous thinking about the fact that you're now with Mom
But your absence makes me saddened
I know Daddy how eagerly you been waiting to meet Mom in heaven
I also know you and mom had a grand reunion after being apart for several years
Knowing all that I still miss you Daddy so very much so very often
I want to tell the world I love my dad in my own way
in my eyes Daddy you were such a rare angel that no money could ever buy
Daddy you were always my loving hero and I was your pampered child
In my eyes you are such a rare angel that no money could ever buy
My love for you Daddy is blind because it's true love
Daddy you were so loving, so gentle, so kind
In my eyes you were such a rare angel that no money could ever buy
So, I won't shed tears today, I won't close my mind today and I won't feel empty today
I will smile, love and go on because I know that's you would want me to do
Because Daddy you were such a rare angel that no money could ever buy

(First published June 16, 2024 Kingsport Times News)

Dr Ramesh Khanna, Dr Tapasi Saha, Dr Karl D Nolph

About The Author

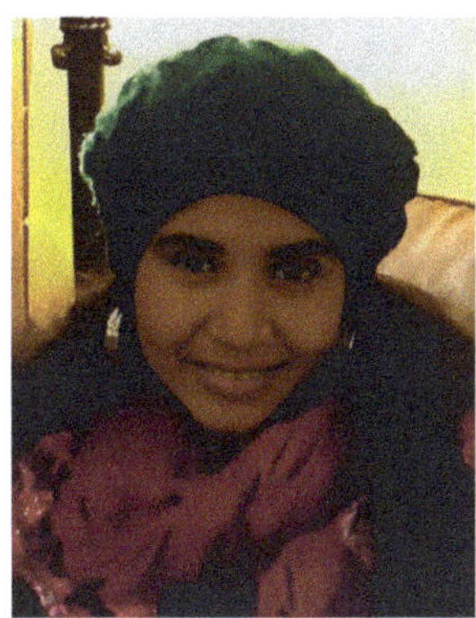

Tapasi Chowdhury Saha MD, FASN, is a board-certified nephrologist and internal medicine doctor. A graduate of one of the nation's top nephrology programs, the University of Missouri, Columbia, she was trained by several of the world's leading nephrologists including Dr. Karl D. Nolph, the pioneer of Peritoneal Dialysis, Dr. Ramesh Khanna, Dr. Gary Ream and Dr. ZJ Twardowskii, inventor of the swan neck peritoneal dialysis catheter.

After completing her nephrology fellowship under the direction of Dr. Nolph, Tapasi joined the nephrology faculty at the East Carolina University Brody School of Medicine as an assistant professor. Seven years later she moved to Tennessee to begin her work in private practice at Regional Kidney Care. She is currently part of the clinical faculties at East Tennessee State University and Lincoln Memorial University.

In addition to her work as a physician, Tapasi is a poet, writer and recital artist. Her poetry has been published both locally and internationally and she has received multiple awards for her writing and recitation.

Tapasi currently resides in Kingsport Tennessee with her husband Pabitra Saha who is an interventional cardiologist. They have two sons, Upal, co-founder of the AI startup Bem, and Dipaul, a student at Georgia State University of Law.

When not at work as a physician or writing poetry, Tapasi enjoys running and cooking.

Tapasi's wish to help her patients is fulfilled in the publishing of this book. Proceeds from the sale of this book are donated to The National Kidney Foundation.

Acknowledgments

I would like to thank the following people:

Trudy Peters, children's book author, who inspired me to publish this book. My life changed the day I met Trudy. She is the most amazingly talented woman I have ever met.

Markelene Earles is the practice manager of Regional Kidney Care. She always helps me with my poetry and keeps a file of my poems on her computer so they are always available to print for patients.

Amber Dingus encourages me and loves to decorate my poetry with different designs.

Trish Berry, my dear friend who always encourages me to write more.

Alicia Canter, BSN, RN and Diane Sporole, BSN, RN, for their ongoing support.

Dave Turner for guiding me through the publishing process and for creating the designs for this book.

Upal and Dipaul Saha, my sons, for joyfully cheering me on.

Pabitra Saha, my beloved husband, for continually supporting my passion for poetry.

Love,
Tapasi

Visit Tapasi on YouTube

https://www.youtube.com/@tapasisaha7577

National
Kidney
Foundation®

The National Kidney Foundation is
revolutionizing the fight to save lives by
eliminating preventable kidney
disease, accelerating innovation for
the dignity of the patient experience,
and dismantling structural inequities
in kidney care, dialysis,
and transplantation.

100% of the profits

from the sale of this book

are donated to the

National Kidney Foundation.

For more information

or to make a donation, please visit:

kidney.org

Index of Poems

Index of Poems